Dear Paul,

What you are [...] respectful ar[...] have a great [...] and weight on our shoulders knowing that you are protecting the United States of America and your Military brothers and sisters. So I found this book that I believe will bring you strength and courage during those times of uncertainty. I also hope that it will keep your faith strong in the protector of all and that is your Lord. When you are finished with your tour of duty please pass this book to one of your fellow military friend and write a small letter of encouragement in it. I Love you and you are always in my prayers.

Love,
Melanie

For God so loved the world, that he gave his only begotten Son, that whosoever believeth in him should not perish, but have everlasting life.

~ John 3:16

BIBLE PROMISES FOR SOLDIERS

J.M. Barnes

authorHOUSE®

AuthorHouse™
1663 Liberty Drive, Suite 200
Bloomington, IN 47403
www.authorhouse.com
Phone: 1-800-839-8640

First published by AuthorHouse 3/25/2008

ISBN: 978-1-4343-3757-3 (sc)

Printed in the United States of America
Bloomington, Indiana

This book is printed on acid-free paper.

Cover designed by J.M. Barnes

ACKNOWLEDGMENTS

There are several people in my life that I have to thank for helping me with this book. First and foremost to my heavenly father, I count it an honor to have been given such a task. Thank you for trusting me enough to give me the idea and the vision for this book. I was not sure I could handle such a great responsibility but I gained more confidence and was able to make this dream a reality because you guided me every step of the way.

To my family, thank you for believing in me and encouraging me to complete my first book.

To my three wonderful children, who worked with me on this project, you are the best. Thanks for reading my many drafts, correcting my errors and giving me your honest opinion. Your positive attitude and enthusiasm was contagious, thank you for all of your hard work. I love you more than you will ever know. I gave birth to you, but you helped me give birth to this book. I look forward to working with you on future projects.

DEDICATION

I dedicate this book to all the brave service men and women of the United States Armed Forces past, present and future. Whenever our nation needs you, you are there. No matter the time or day, you are there to protect our interest both foreign and domestic. As a citizen, I know I can depend on you to defend and protect our nation. Our nation would pay a great price if it were not for your sacrifice and service. Because of your sacrifice, I now live in a world secure in peace. I do not take my freedom for granted. Thank you for having the courage of heart to answer the call and for standing up and fighting for my freedom and liberty. I applaud your dedication and selfless service to our nation.

I want to thank you for answering the call to serve and protect our country. You have made it possible for all the citizens of this great nation to enjoy freedom. Generations yet to be born will enjoy freedom and live a life free from fear and terror. You have left a legacy of honor and integrity for your families that will live on from generation to generation.

It is the soldier, not the reporter, who has given us freedom of the press.

It is the soldier, not the poet, who has given us freedom of speech.

It is the soldier, not the organizer, who has given us the freedom to demonstrate.

It is the soldier, who salutes the flag, who serves beneath the flag,

And whose coffin is draped by the flag, who allows the protestor to burn the flag.

By: Father Denis Edward O'Brien M.M. USMC

CONTENTS

INTRODUCTION

The first war that ever took place did not take place on earth. The first war took place over two thousand years ago in heaven. This war was not between mortal beings. This war was between a host of angelic beings. It was the classic clash between good and evil, creator versus creation. It was God versus Lucifer. The war started because Lucifer the angel became full of pride and decided to exalt himself above God. It was not enough for him to be on the Holy mountain of God, he wanted to establish his own kingdom in heaven and become God.

The bible states *"Lucifer was the seal of perfection, full of wisdom and perfect in beauty. He was an anointed, beautiful cherub who had instruments built inside of him and precious jewels as his covering".*

However, he became so full of pride that he devised a plan to exalt himself over God. He was able to convince a large number of angels to form an alliance with him to take over God's kingdom. This was the beginning of the first war ever fought. In the end, Lucifer and his host of angels were not able to prevail. He and his angels were expelled out of heaven as quick as lightening flashing across the sky. Isaiah 14 and Ezekiel 28 both give an account of what happened to Lucifer because of his rebellion.

I mention this story because so many people have the idea that wars only exist between humans. Some believe God is not in favor of war to resolve conflicts and that he is only interested in peaceful negotiations. There is no question; it is the will of God that we live a quiet and peaceful life. However, sometimes war is the only way in which peace can be achieved. Once peace is achieved, sometimes war is the only means by which peace can be maintained. George Washington said it best when he said, "To be prepared for war is one of the most effective means of preserving peace." I know talking about war makes some people uncomfortable because war is not pretty. There will surely be bloodshed, sorrow, pain and even death.

However, in Matthew 24, Jesus himself in talking with his disciples said, in the last days there will be wars and rumors of war. Nation will rise against nation, and kingdoms against kingdoms. We now live in the day in which Jesus spoke of when talking to his disciples. There have been wars fought in the past between countries, and our country is currently engaged in two major wars. One in Iraq, the other in Afghanistan and there will be wars to fight in the future. When God wanted inhabitants driven out of the land, he assigned the task to the military.

When God wanted his will and purpose established, he has always used the military to accomplish his will and purpose on the earth. Our military today is no different from the military of old, except the weapons of warfare are different. The military in the Old Testament used swords, spears, bow and arrows. There were some soldiers in the military who were trained to use slings and rocks.

The military today is a lot more sophisticated than in the past. The weapons that the military uses today are ships, airplanes, guns, tanks, bombs and other weapons too numerous to list. There are some soldiers in the military who are trained and assigned to special military units. Their missions and assignments are top secret and unknown to them, their family and friends.

The bible is steep in military history and tradition. It is also filled with military battle strategies. Some of the great military leaders of the past depended on the bible for wisdom as they laid out their battle plan and prepared to go to war. God has always been involved in military affairs. Those who asked him for wisdom and direction before a battle always came out on top. He is the ultimate Commander and Chief.

Men and women join the military and take the oath to serve for different reasons. Some because they are carrying on a family tradition, while others see the military as their only option for a better life. Many men and women join for personal reasons like earning money for college or helping their family who is struggling financially. Others join to travel and see the world. However, many men and women join the military out of a sense of duty to God and their country.

These men and women know they are called to serve in the military. They know the training is hard and they will work long hours without any overtime pay. They realize they will not see their families and friends for months and in some cases years. However, none of these things deters them or shakes their belief that what they are doing is what they were called to do.

While politicians argue and debate the war, questioning if we should be in Iraq and Afghanistan, the troops are preparing for deployment. They are training and preparing themselves physically and mentally for the battles that lie ahead. They are committed to answering the call no matter the cost. The joy of a service member's commitment to God and country outweighs the fear of war, injury and even death.

Their commitment to the mission, fellow soldiers and the nation goes beyond all fear because they want to accomplish the mission and see it succeed. Politics are not an issue when you are engaged in combat. Political affiliations and parties lines are irrelevant. Soldiers do not care if their comrade to the right or left of them is a Republican, Democratic or Independent. They do not care what their comrade's religious affiliation is. They will do whatever it takes to keep each other from harm and together defeat their enemies.

Soldiers know going into the military that they will face hardships and they are willing to endure the hardships. In the bible 2 Timothy chapter 2 verses 3 and 4 *(amplified bible)* says, "Therefore endure hardship as a good soldier of Jesus Christ. No soldier when in service becomes entangled in the enterprises of (civilian) life; his aim is to satisfy and please the one who enlisted him."

When a service member is on the battlefield, he or she does not concern himself or herself with civilian life. Their commanders tell them before deploying to the war zone to give someone they trust power of attorney to handle their affairs while they are away. Leaders know soldiers cannot afford to be distracted in combat, thinking about the electric or water bill while on the battlefield. Their aim and goal is to satisfy and please the one who enlisted them. They want success in battle, and they want to return to their home and loved ones safe and sound.

Ecclesiastes 3 says, "There is an appointed time for everything and there is a time for every event under heaven. Verse 8 says, there is a time to love, and a time to hate; a time for war and a time for peace." There is a time and season for everything in life including war. If you are preparing for your time of war, know that God is there to protect you, guide you and keep you.

UNDERSTANDING THE
CALL TO THE NATIONS

Over the years, I have looked at many men and women in uniform and thought to myself, "Why did they join the military?" I found it hard to believe that someone would volunteer to put him or herself in harm's way.   I did not understand why someone would go to the recruiter's office and join the military, especially in times of war. However, a few years ago, I discovered the answer to my question, in the bible.

As my husband prepared to go to Iraq, I was very concerned about his safety. He had already served in the first Gulf war and I wanted him to retire. As he prepared for the war, he became totally focused on physically and mentally preparing himself for the mission. I discovered that men and women who join the military are called to the military.

As the wife of a soldier, it took a long time for me to recognize and understand the call my husband has on his life. In fact, I had to realize that for him, being in the military is not just a job it is a calling. I had always assumed that if someone said, I have been called, they were talking about being called to minister in a church.

However, not every calling means a person will be a pastor of a church, preaching in the pulpit every Sunday. There are men and women who are called to service, and their job is to serve their country. They have answered the call and taken an oath to serve and protect their country.

Soldiers are called not only to protect their country; they are called to be ambassadors for their nation. According to Webster's dictionary, the word ambassador means, *an important person who represents his or her country in another country.* Soldiers travel and live all over the world and in each country they reside in, they still have to represent their country in a professional and positive way.

Soldiers are not only ambassadors for their country, but they are ambassadors for Jesus Christ. They are God's hands extended to others in need. Another definition for the word ambassador is envoy, which Webster defines as *messenger or agent a diplomatic representative who is dispatched on a special mission.*

Luke chapter 14 verses 31 and 32 says, "Or what king, going out to engage in conflict with another king, will not first sit down and consider and take counsel whether he is able with ten thousand to meet him who comes against him with twenty thousand? And if he cannot do so, when the other king is still a great way off, he sends an envoy and asks the terms of peace". Matthew chapter 5 verse 9 says, "Blessed are the peacemakers, for they shall be called sons of God."

Soldiers not only train for warfare and combat, they are trained to establish peace as well. Soldiers restore order where there is chaos and disorder. They bring peace where there is trouble. They restore hope to hopeless situations. They assist others by bringing humanitarian aide to those who are suffering and in need.

In the book of 2 Chronicles chapter 17 verses 16, there was a warrior by the name of Amasiah. The bible says, he freely volunteered himself along with 200,000 men and he regarded this as his service to the Lord. He counted it an honor to volunteer and serve in the military.

David volunteered himself to serve in the military also. His father gave him the responsibility of watching the flock and carrying food to his brothers who were in the military. David was also King Saul's armor-bearer and musician. However, when he heard Goliath taunting, threatening, and disgracing the army of Israel for over forty days he made a decision.

David left his father's sheep with a shepherd keeper, laid down his harp and volunteered himself to fight Goliath. Although David faced opposition from his brothers, he did not let that stop him from volunteering to fight. He said to King Saul, "let no man's heart fail because of him, your servant will go and fight with this Philistine."

David was a young boy, but he was confident and he was courageous. He knew that if he did not kill Goliath, the children of Israel and the army of God would be fighting with this philistine generation after generation. This meant his children, grandchildren and great grandchildren would have to fight the philistines.

Therefore, David took his shepherd's staff, five smooth stones and a sling and he went after Goliath. David not only defeated Goliath, he used Goliath's own sword to cut off his head and gave it to King Saul. David made sure this philistine Goliath would never come against the army of God again and he made sure future generations would not have to deal with him either. In addition to killing Goliath, David fought and killed several of Goliath's brothers as well.

After David became King, he needed help building his army. Several men volunteered and joined his army. Each day more and more men volunteered and joined David's army until he had a huge army. The bible says, "They were mighty men, helpers in the war. They were skillful warriors who could use both their right and left hands in battle."

Other mighty men joined David's army as well. The bible describes them as *mighty men of valor. Men trained for war, fit for battle whose faces were like the faces of lions and who were as fast as gazelles.* As I read this passage of scripture in 1 Chronicles chapter 7, describing these warriors, three words jumped off the page at me. The words trained, fit, and speed. They were not only skilled with their hands, they were physically fit and combat ready.

Just as Amasiah, David, and many other men of war volunteered to serve in the military, there are men and women who have volunteered themselves by enlisting in the military today. They have made a commitment to God, and to their country. They have answered a very high calling. This calling requires that they be willing to lose their life.

Psalms 110 verse 3 says, "your people shall be willing in the day of thy power, in the beauties of holiness from the womb of the morning: thou hast the dew of thy youth." The New international version of that scripture says,

"Your troops will be willing on your day of battle." The word willing means they will volunteer themselves, they will enlist to fight the Lord's battle.

What an awesome display of sacrifice and service to God and country. What would our lives, our country and countries around the world be like without the military? What would happen if no one answered the call to enlist, serve his or her country, and serve God? We surely would not be able to enjoy the peace, freedom, and liberties we have today. I am grateful to all the men and women who have volunteered and answered the call to serve in the military.

Not only did God use men in battle in the Old Testament, he used women as well. I have been around the military for more than twenty years. I know in some cases women have a hard time in the military. Many experience increased hardships when it is time to go to war. Some of the males in their unit think they are not capable of fighting in a war. Many male soldiers have said, and believe that women should not be in the military at all.

They believe that women should not go to war, because they are a liability in combat. However, God does not think so. There is no respect of persons with him. God used many women in the bible during times of war. God used a woman by the name of Deborah, she was a prophetess, judge and a military advisor. God gave Deborah the battle plan to give to Barak. He was the commander of the army.

Barak did not question what Deborah said, he did not ignore her advice. He gladly received what she told him and he immediately obeyed her words.

The word God told Deborah to give to Barak was "go to war against the Canaanites." Take ten thousand soldiers from the tribes of Zebulun and Naphtali, march to Mount Tabor and fight against Sisera the commander of the army. Deborah told Barak in advance God would give Sisera into his hand. Barak was so confident in Deborah that he told Deborah he would only go to war against the Canaanites if she went with them. Barak had a high level of respect for Deborah and her position as a judge, leader and military advisor.

Deborah was a very courageous, confident leader. The bible does not say that she broke down in tears at Barak's request because she was afraid to go to war. On the contrary, she said, "I will surely go with you." She also told Barak the glory of the battle would not go to him but it would go to a woman instead. This statement did not offend Barak. He did not care who got the glory in this battle. He just wanted his army to win.

I know there are leaders who are gender bias when it comes to fighting in wars. However, God is not gender bias. He will use whoever makes him or herself available to him whether male or female. The woman Deborah was referring to was a woman by the name of Jael. She was of the clan of the Kenites and she dwelled in a tent with her husband Heber. She was immortalized for her bravery in the face of danger.

In Judges Chapter 5 Sisera, the general of the Canaanite army was in the mist of a fierce battle with the Israelites. The bible says, " God caused him to become confused and frightened during the battle." Sisera jumped off his chariot and ran on foot toward the tent of Jael. When she saw him coming, she told him to come into her tent and she covered him with a mantle, which is a blanket or rug. After he fell asleep, she took a tent peg and hammer then she drove it through his temple killing him. God gave the battle plan to a woman, he spoke a word through a woman, and he used a woman to defeat the enemy in battle.

She did not kill someone untrained in warfare. She killed a mighty man of valor, a general in the Canaanite army. In the latter part of Judges Chapter 5, Deborah and Barak sang a song thanking God for giving them victory in battle saying, Praise ye the Lord for the avenging of Israel, when the people willingly offered themselves. Zebulun and Naphtali were people who jeopardized or endangered their lives unto the death. One translation of the bible says, the word jeopardized in the Hebrew means they were exposed to reproach. While others gave reasons and excuses why they could not go to war, these soldiers were willing to endure criticism, disapproval and blame to answer the call and fight.

There is another account in the book of Judges Chapter 9 where God used a woman to defeat his enemy. The bible does not give us her name, it just says, "A certain woman." The woman heard that Abimelech, who was one of the sons of Gideon, had hired men to kill his brothers. He had 70 brothers and he had all of them killed. After having all of his brothers slaughtered, Abimelech headed toward this woman's city. When the woman heard he was coming to her city, she knew his plan was to kill everyone in her city. She decided to hide in a fortified tower and wait for Abimelech to arrive.

When she saw Abimelech preparing to burn down the tower, she dropped a millstone on Abimelech's head, crushing his skull and severely wounding him. Abimelech did not want it recorded in history that a woman killed him, so he told his armor bearer to kill him. Here again, God used a woman in a time of war to bring justice and to save an entire city.

In the book of 2 Samuel chapter 20 God used another woman to defeat an enemy and save her entire city. The bible does not give us her name either. It just refers to her as "a wise woman." Joab, the commander of David's army was pursuing a man by the name of Sheba. Sheba had caused a revolt against David. Sheba had also convinced some of David's men to leave and follow him instead.

David had already experienced a similar situation with his son Absalom and he did not want to go through another revolt. Therefore, he instructed Joab the commander of his army to find Sheba before he could find a fortified city and escape. Joab gathered the soldiers and went to the city. After Joab arrived with the soldiers to the city, he instructed them to build a siege ramp to gain access to the city. When the woman saw what was happening, she cried out to Joab. She asked Joab if she could have a word with him. Joab agreed to her request and went to talk to her.

She said, "I am one of the peaceful and faithful in Israel, do you intend to kill a mother of Israel?" Joab responded to her by telling her he did not want to kill her or destroy her city. He just wanted Sheba handed over to him and he and the army would depart. The woman in her wisdom went to the people in her city and advised them to give Joab the head of Sheba so the city could be spared from destruction.

 The people agreed and someone found Sheba, cut off his head and threw it over the wall to Joab. Joab blew the trumpet, which was a signal for the soldiers to retreat. This woman was able to negotiate with a military leader and save her entire city. Again, God is not gender bias. He will use a woman or a man if they make themselves available to do his will.

GOD ORDAINED THE MILITARY

I know war is not a popular subject in our culture today. There will always be people who will protest against the military and war. Some may feel they are doing God's will when they march and protest against war. I am not here to judge anyone or say they are wrong, because we are all entitled to our own opinion. However, I would like to remind those who protest of something very important.

It was the blood, sweat, and tears of men and women who fought and were willing to die for their country, who gave them the right to protest. Their sacrifice has given all of us the freedom to voice our opinion. Many people think God is against the military and war. They think the military originated with man or was man's idea however, that is not true. There are many stories in the bible about the military or the armies of God. Many battles were planned, ordained, and orchestrated by the hand of God.

God used the military to fight his battles, destroy his enemies and defend his people. When reading the Old Testament, I noticed that in almost every chapter there was some type of battle. Most of the Old Testament is about war. In the book of Exodus, God told the children of Israel to leave Egypt where they were slaves. He gave the children of Israel a promise that he would lead them to Canaan the promise land. However, before the children of Israel could inherit the land God promised them, they had to fight and drive out the people who were in the land.

Freedom from bondage and slavery meant they had to fight and remove the squatters who were in their land of promise. God needed an army to accomplish this task, so he became a recruiter; In fact, God was the first military recruiter. In Numbers 1:3 God instructed Moses to take a census of the children of Israel.

He told Moses to count the number of men who were 20 years of age and over who were able to go to war. Moses obeyed the Lord and when Moses finished the census, the army numbered 603,550 men. As soon as God gave the command, the soldiers went into action and they destroyed all of their enemies. God could have used angels to remove the inhabitants from the land, but he used the military instead.

Many people may not believe it, but soldiers are servants of God. In the book of Numbers chapter 31 verses 1 through 6, God again instructed Moses to send recruiters to the twelve tribes of Israel. He recruited soldiers to fight against the Midianites. It is worth noting that Moses said, "Arm some of yourselves for war". Not all of the men of Israel were recruited just a select number of men from each of the twelve tribes were recruited. There were one thousand men from each of the twelve tribes. They were the brave, the courageous, and they were called "men of war." The men of war never went to war alone. God went with them. God is "A MAN OF WAR".

God is and always will be the ultimate Commander and Chief. In the book of Exodus chapter 15 verses 3-7, Moses wrote a song describing God's actions in battle.

The Lord is a warrior; The Lord is his name. Pharaoh's chariots and his army he has cast into the sea and the choicest of his officers are drowned in the Red sea. The deep covers them; they went down into the depths like a stone. Your right hand, O Lord, is majestic in power, your right hand, O Lord, shatters the enemy and the greatness of your excellence you overthrow those who rise up against you; You sent forth your burning anger, and it consumed them like a chaff.

In Deuteronomy chapter 20, the army of Israel was given the Laws of Warfare. The first thing God wanted to eliminate from the heart of the soldiers was fear. He knew that if their hearts were full of fear, they would lose every battle. Fear would overtake them and their enemies would defeat them.

The Laws of Warfare states," *when you go out to battle against your enemies and see horses and chariots and people more numerous than you, do not be afraid of them; for the Lord your God, who brought you up from the land of Egypt, is with you. When you are approaching the battle, the priest shall come near and speak to the people. He shall say to them, Hear O Israel, you are approaching the battle against your enemies today. Do not be fainthearted, do not be afraid or panic or tremble before them. For the Lord your God is the one who goes with you, to fight for you against your enemies to save you."*

(New American Standard)

After the death of Moses, the first thing God told Joshua after he took the position as commander of the army was "be strong and courageous." He said those words to Joshua three times in the first chapter of the book of Joshua. This was not something he suggested to Joshua, he commanded Joshua to be strong and courageous. This was a military order. God knows how important it is for soldiers to have a fearless heart. You cannot win a battle if you are fearful. Some things are contagious and carry a scent. Fear is one of those things. Your enemy will use your fear against you and defeat you. Each time Joshua prepared for battle against his enemy, God would speak to him and say, "Do not be afraid".

Faith is also contagious, and God knew he had to establish faith in the heart of Joshua if he was going to command the army and win battles. After Joshua received that command from the Lord, he went throughout the camp and encouraged the people telling them to be strong and courageous. God gave the strategy and battle plan to Joshua and Joshua obeyed and defeated his enemy.

One of the maneuvers God told Joshua and others to use was to hamstring or lame the horses and burn the chariots. He knew the enemy could not escape if their horses and chariots where destroyed. They would have to run away on foot, or they would have to stay and fight. God is not a coward and he does not like coward soldiers.

If a soldier became fearful, there was someone in position to encourage him. This person had a very important position in the military. It was the position of being the priest. Some people may think the role of the priest is not important in the military or in combat. However, that is not true. Due to a lack of understanding, the role of the priest during combat is underestimated and the position is not valued. Many miracles took place in the bible when the priest went to war with the soldiers. They are not called priest any more they are called chaplains. The name has changed but their role is just as important today as it was years ago. While reading some of the stories in the Old Testament, I read about a priest who was one of David's right hand men. In 1 Chronicles 12, the bible gives us his name. His name is Zadok and his name means "righteous".

Zadok was not only a priest he was a warrior in the army as well. The bible describes him as a valiant warrior. He was loyal to David and to God in his performance of duties. God rewarded him for his service and loyalty by establishing his name in history. When Solomon, David's son began his reign as king, he appointed Azariah the son of Zadok to the position of high priest. God rewarded Zadok and he rewarded his descendants as well.

The way God rewarded Zadok was by allowing Zadok's descendants to keep the priesthood under their control. This priest left a long legacy of honor for his children and grandchildren. Just as God instructed the priest to go into battle with the soldiers in the Old Testament, the priest goes into battle with soldiers today. These modern day priests known as chaplains are a vital part of the military and the mission.

Chaplains are a source of spiritual strength and encouragement. God knew that soldiers would get tired and weary during war. Therefore, he placed someone in position in the military to encourage and support the soldiers who are on the battlefield. They join soldiers on combat patrols and missions, and pray with soldiers on the battlefield.

Chaplains bring words of comfort and joy to those who are lonely. Chaplains are there to help soldiers overcome any fears or worries they may have as they go into battle to face their enemies. They provide the spiritual food they need for strength as well. They encourage the discouraged. They pray for the injured and they honor the dead. Even after war, Chaplains are there to provide prayer and counseling to soldiers and their families who are having difficulty after deployment.

Although chaplains do not carry a physical weapon like a gun, they do carry a spiritual weapon that is more powerful, which is the word of God. Hebrews 4 says, "For the word of God is quick, and powerful and sharper than any two-edged sword."

In the Old Testament, the priest would give the battle cry by blowing the shofar horn and the soldiers would begin to fight. Now, soldiers have another priest who goes into battle with them as well. He is our present high priest and he is Jesus Christ.

In the book of Joshua chapter 5, starting at verse 13, and ending in chapter 6, the Captain of the Army of God showed up at Gilgal to talk to Joshua. The Captain came with his sword drawn in his hand, which means he came to fight.

"And it came to pass, when Joshua was by Jericho, that he lifted His eyes and looked, and behold, a Man stood opposite him with his sword drawn in his hand. And Joshua went to him and said to him,

"Are you for us or for our adversaries?" So he said, "No; rather I indeed come now as captain of the host of the Lord." And Joshua fell on his face to the earth, bowed down, and said to him, "What has my Lord to say to his servant?" The captain of the Lord's host said to Joshua, "Remove your sandals from your foot, for the place where you stand is holy."

(New American Standard)

As Joshua listened, the Captain gave him the battle plan and strategy he would need to defeat his enemy. Joshua obeyed the instructions he was given and he and his soldiers won the battle. Part of the battle plan was to have seven-priest blow the ram or shofar horn. This is the story of Joshua and the walls of Jericho coming down. I believe the Captain of God's Army brought an angelic host of beings that Joshua could not see.

They tore down the walls of Jericho when the army gave a mighty shout! I know it is hard for people to think of God as a man of war because we are so accustomed to hearing that God is a God of love and peace. That is true; however, there is another side of his divine nature that we do not always talk about. That is the warrior side of his nature. He knows how to fight and win battles. In the Old Testament whenever God wanted inhabitants driven out of the land, he used the military to do it.

God used the military to carry out his plans, so his will and purpose could be established on the earth. It might sound cruel but there were times when God instructed the leaders of the army not to take anyone captive. In fact, in many cases he said, kill everything. God told the soldiers to kill all the cattle, men, women, and children.

God wanted to make sure the captives did not bring their pagan beliefs and rituals into the camp of the Israelites. God used the military then and he uses the military now. The weapons and methods are different, but the purpose is still the same. "Thy kingdom come, thy will be done." God is a God of mercy and grace, but he is also a "MAN OF WAR."

THE ENTITLEMENTS OF WAR

Some professions will never pay the person what they are worth. In my opinion, the military is one of those jobs. I know this might be a controversial statement but being a military spouse, I know first hand what it is like to live from paycheck to paycheck. I feel those who are willing to serve in the military should be the highest paid professionals in the country. Unfortunately, that is not the case. We live in a society that places more value on entertainment.

Athletes and Hollywood celebrities are the heroes and idols, not the men and women fighting and dying on the battlefield. Companies and corporations pay athletes and movie stars millions of dollars a year to entertain us. We pay doctors tens of thousand of dollars to diagnose us and help us live a long healthy life. We pay lawyers thousands to defend us in court. However, some service members barely earn minimum wage and they are willing to lay down their lives to protect us. It is sad but it is true, there are many junior enlisted soldiers with families living below the poverty level. Some of these families qualify for government assistance. Many service members are injured in combat and are denied disability claims and proper health care. That is shameful in my opinion.

Service members are willing to sacrifice their lives to protect their country and its citizens. They are willing to die so others can live in peace. I have not met a movie star or professional athlete who is willing to die for me. The only person who was willing to die for humanity was Jesus Christ. That is why I believe men and women in uniform are servants of God. When someone is willing to give their life for their country and humanity, they are following the example of Jesus Christ. You cannot put a price on someone's life.

While reading about the great warriors in the bible, one thing continued to jump out at me. They were all wealthy. I saw a pattern emerge in all of their lives that I could not ignore. They were all wealthy because they went to war and fought the Lord's battles. These soldiers received certain entitlements that made them wealthy. Some of the heroes and warriors in the bible were men like Abraham, Joshua, Caleb and David to name a few.

God made sure these men received proper compensation for their military service by giving them the spoils of battle. Not only were they compensated financially, God made their names great. Some of these great warriors are honorably mentioned in Hebrews chapter 11 verse 32. Their names are listed among those in the great hall of faith. I saw this principle of compensation, as I like to call it throughout the bible, as I examined the lives of the Old and New Testament warriors. Let's take a look at a few of them. In Genesis chapters 14 and 15, Abraham took 318-trained men and defeated several kings. As a result, God gave Abraham the spoils of that battle and God made Abraham the father of many nations.

Next, there was Gideon in the book of Judges chapter 8, who initially was a timid man, hiding in his father's winepress from the Midianites. God used him to defeat the Midianites. After Gideon defeated the Midianites, he took back everything his enemies stole from his people. He even took the pendants and crescent ornaments that were on the necks of the camels. In one battle he took over 43 pounds of gold earrings and God made his name great.

Then there is the story of David who killed Goliath in the valley of Elah in 1 Samuel chapter 17. After killing Goliath with a simple sling and a rock, David was promoted by the king. King Saul set him over the men of war, and even gave David his daughter as a wife. Eventually, God anointed David to become the King of Israel. David had a son named Solomon who became a great warrior as well. Solomon's army was known for its chariots. In 1 Kings chapter 9, Solomon had so many chariots, he needed cities to store them in. Solomon was also known for his wisdom and his wealth. He was probably the richest man in history.

In 2 Samuel 23 David listed his mighty men of valor. These men were very loyal to David. On one occasion, David had been running from King Saul because Saul wanted to kill him. He was extremely tired and thirsty. He made a comment to his men saying, "I wish I had a drink of water". Without hesitation, three of David's bravest warriors risked their lives by going through the camp of their enemy the philistines. They were not afraid to do whatever it took to get water from a well for their commander. David was so humbled by their loyalty, dedication and willingness to jeopardize their life that he decided he could not drink the water. He poured the water on the ground as an offering to the Lord instead.

All these men were warriors, but they were not poor warriors. God rewarded them for their sacrifice and service. Now I know there are entitlements soldiers receive when they deploy and I know our government does not allow soldiers to acquire or keep the goods of battle. However, I believe there is a special blessing that rest upon every soldier and his or her family for their sacrifices and service to their country. God is faithful and he will not forget the sacrifice and labor of those who fight for their country.

THE COST OF FREEDOM

There is no higher calling than to serve others and many have paid the ultimate price to answer the call. If you have lost a comrade, friend or loved one in any war, their sacrifice and service did not escape the eyes of God. He is a righteous God. He has not forgotten those who have laid down their lives to see his will established in the earth. Take pride in their service to their nation. Cherish their memory and their legacy. Remember, in God's eyes he or she did not die in vain.

Proverbs chapter 10 verse 7 says, "The memory of the righteous is blessed." Be proud of the fact that he or she answered the call, and was willing to die for their country and the cause of freedom. It has become just a cliché for some, but it is a fact that freedom is not free. In John chapter 15 verse 13, the scripture says of Jesus, "Greater love has no one than this, than to lay down one's life for his friends". Jesus Christ became our example by shedding his blood and dying on the cross for our sins so he could redeem humanity and give us eternal life. Many soldiers have followed the example of Jesus. They have shed their blood and laid down their lives so we can enjoy the freedoms we have today.

In 2 Samuel chapter 1, there is the story of David and his best friend Jonathan, the son of King Saul. Jonathan's father tried many times to capture and kill David. However, Jonathan and David made a covenant to protect each other and they kept their promise to each other. When David received word that Jonathan was killed in battle, he tore his clothes, wept bitterly and mourned his death. During his time of mourning, David wrote a song that can be found in 2 Samuel chapter 1 verses 21-27, the title of the song is "The Song of the Bow." David told the men who were with him to teach the song to the children of Judah.   You really get a sense of how much he loved Jonathan when he wrote this song.

> *The shield of the mighty is cast away…*
> *They were swifter than eagles, they were stronger than lions…*
> *How the mighty have fallen in the midst of the battle…*
> *I am distressed for, my brother Jonathan; you have been*
> *pleasant to me…*
> *Your love for me was wonderful, surpassing the love of women…*

These two warriors had an extraordinary relationship. The bible says, David grieved and mourned for Jonathan. That means David literally tore out his hair, beat his chest and wailed for Jonathan. However, at some point David realized as much as it hurt to lose his best friend, he had to move forward with his life. He never forgot Jonathan, he would always miss his presence, but he could not mourn forever, there were other battles to fight.

In the book of Isaiah chapter 61 verse 3 it says, "He will console those who mourn in Zion, give them beauty for ashes, the oil of joy for mourning, and the garment of praise for the spirit of heaviness."   Psalm 30, the latter part of verse 5 says, "Weeping may endure for a night, but joy comes in the morning." If you have lost someone dear to you, God will give you the strength and power to move on with your life. He has promised to never leave you nor forsake you.

The cost of war does not only include the loss of comrades. It often includes the loss of relationships. Many engagements and marriages are unable to stand under the weight of a deployment and in some cases multiple deployments. The stress on the relationship becomes unbearable for some couples.

Finally, we owe Jesus a debt we can never repay him for sacrificing his life, shedding his blood and dying on the cross for our sins. Likewise, we owe our service men and women a debt we can never repay them. They have and are sacrificing their lives, shedding their blood and dying on the battlefield for humanity. Although, they did not die on a physical cross, many tombstones in Arlington National Cemetery and cemeteries around the world bear the symbol of the cross. These symbols serve to remind us of their faith and the price that they paid for our freedom.

Coincidence?

I think not.

I think it is divine.

RECOVERY FROM WAR

David was perhaps the most famous bible warrior of all times. He had a very illustrious military career. I think the reason David was so successful, was because he asked God for wisdom before going into battle. He listened to the advice of the priest and his commanders. He remained humble giving God glory and not seeking his own. He sought the face of God in times of uncertainty, he gave God credit for giving him victory in every battle. God was the person who kept him from harm and death. David did not fight in just one or two battles during his military career he was constantly fighting battles.

David faced everything imaginable during those times. Every year the king would go out to battle. He would not sit on his throne and let the soldiers do all the fighting. He went to war also, knowing his neck literally was on the line. To kill the king and cut off his head was a true sign of victory for the military. It would surely boost the soldiers' morale and confidence to have the head of a king. It was a sure sign of defeat for their enemy. In most cases, the army would run in fear once the king was killed. When David became King God protected him each time he went to war.

I think David found the key that help him recover from war. In the book of 2 Samuel chapter 22, David wrote a song of praise thanking God for delivering him from the hand of all his enemies. David knew that the Lord was responsible for giving him victory in battle. As I looked at the lives of other Old Testament warriors, I noticed they used music, songs and poetry to help them recover from war. They wrote and sang about their battles, and they wrote and sang songs about God's deliverance. Music had a very calming effect on those returning from war. When King Saul could not sleep and became troubled, he would call for the musician. Before David became a soldier, he was Saul's musician. He would play his harp for Saul and Saul would calm down. Even David, had moments of distress. He had to hide in caves when his enemies pursued him. His son Absalom plotted to kill him and take over his kingdom. As a result, David had to hide from his son Absalom until he was killed. David learned the secret that helped him recover from war, he pinned songs of praise and thanksgiving to God. He wrote Psalm3, when he was fleeing from his son Absalom.

He pinned Psalm 4 when he could not sleep at night. He wrote Psalm 41 when he was in terrible distress. He pinned Psalm 56 after being captured and tormented by the philistines in Gath. David endured everything imaginable during his military career. Even during times of great despair, David learned to encourage himself in the Lord. He had highs and lows and moments when he re-lived the warfare he had experienced. When he found himself getting really depressed, he would remind himself of God's saving grace. He would talk to his soul, which is the seat of our mind, will and emotions. He would ask himself the question, "Why are you cast down my soul?" Trust in the Lord. David's faith, thanksgiving, and praises to God, helped him recover from the memories and trauma of war.

One thing that is troubling to me is the number of service members returning from combat and having a difficult time readjusting to life after combat. One of the weapons satan uses to keep service members in bondage to memories of war is, fear. I know from my husband's experience in Iraq, fear was the thing he struggled with. I had friends tell me their spouses returned from combat a different person. They told me not to be surprised if my husband came back different as well.

Honestly, I did not believe them. I thought that was just their experience. It would not be mine. Boy was I in for a rude awakening. When my husband returned from Iraq, he was quite a ball of emotions. He was very jumpy, irritated, and angry. He had a fear of crowds and bridges. He suffered from insomnia due to flashbacks and nightmares to name a few. It was a very difficult time for our entire family. Fear and Torment are weapons satan uses. However, I believe there is deliverance in Jesus Christ. It is not the will of God for anyone who has fought for their country to have to fight with the memories of war. One scripture says, fear has torment, but perfect love cast out all fear.

The Love of God is able to drive out all fear. The other thing satan uses to keep service members in bondage is silence. There are many reasons for the silence. Most soldiers are too embarrassed to ask for or seek help. Some fear they will seem weak and lose the respect of their comrades, family and friends. Some fear they will lose their position in the military. Some do not know where to go to get the help they need. Others fear they will be stigmatized if they ask for help. This code of silence must be broken. In my case, I knew my husband would not seek help for himself. Therefore, I gently approached the subject with him and I was able to convinced him to talk to someone about what he was experiencing.

I scheduled the appointment and I went with him to his first appointment. Once we got there, I helped him fill out the paperwork. I sat in the initial session with him and listened as he talked about some of his experiences in Iraq. It was hard to listen as he talked about some of the things he had experienced. Nevertheless, it was needful and beneficial for him.

He was diagnosed with Post traumatic stress disorder commonly called PTSD. I can only imagine the number of service members suffering from post -traumatic stress disorder and who need help. I would like to encourage those of you reading this book that have suffered and are currently suffering with some of the things I described earlier to seek help. There is no shame in asking for help. You are a veteran of the United States Armed Services and you are entitled to get the help you need. Do not be reluctant to seek help.

Do not suffer alone.

What is post-traumatic stress disorder?

Post-traumatic stress disorder (PTSD) is a type of anxiety problem. It can develop after your safety or life is threatened, or after you experience or see a traumatic event. Some examples of traumatic events are a natural disaster, rape, severe car crash or fighting in a war. Usually, the event makes you feel very afraid or helpless. People with PTSD have trouble coping with and getting over traumatic events and often feel the effects for months afterward.

Physical activation or arousal

The body's fight-or-flight reaction to a life-threatening situation continues long after the event is over. It is upsetting to feel like your body is overreacting or out of control. However, on the positive side, these fight-or-flight reactions help prepare a person in a dangerous situation for quick response and emergency action. Signs of continuing physical activation, common following participation in war, can include:

- Being startle easily at sudden noise

- Severe headache if thinking of the event

- Sweating

- Having trouble concentrating, indecisiveness

- Upset stomach, trouble eating

- Outbursts of anger

Who develops PTSD?

Whether you will develop PTSD may depend partly on how severe and intense the trauma was and how long it lasted. People who have anxiety, depression or other mental disorders are more likely to develop PTSD. People who have been victims of previous trauma are also at greater risk.

Who is at risk for developing PTSD?

The following people may be at risk for PTSD:

- Anyone who has been victimized

- Anyone who has seen a violent act

- Survivors of rape, domestic violence, physical assault such as a mugging or any other random act of violence

- Survivors of unexpected events such as car wrecks, fires or terrorist attacks

- Survivors of natural disasters such as hurricanes or earthquakes

- Anyone who was sexually or physically abused

- Soldiers, veterans or victims of war or combat

- Anyone who has responded to traumatic events such as firefighters, police or rescue workers

- Anyone diagnosed with a life-threatening illness or those who have had surgery

- Anyone who has experienced grief such as the unexpected loss of a loved one

What are the symptoms of PTSD?

You can have symptoms right after the trauma or they can develop months, or even years, later. Your symptoms may include:

- Having flashbacks (feeling like it is happening again)

- Nightmares, bad memories or hallucinations

- Trying not to think about the trauma or staying away from people who remind you of it

- Not being able to recall parts of the event

- Feeling emotionally numb or detached from others

- Having trouble sleeping

- Being irritable, angry or jumpy

- Distress and physical reactions (e.g., heart pounding, shaking) when reminded of the trauma

People with PTSD are often depressed. Sometimes they try to feel better by using alcohol or drugs. This can lead to substance abuse and addiction.

How is PTSD diagnosed?

Your doctor can diagnose PTSD by talking with you about your symptoms and experiences.

How is PTSD treated?

There are many treatments available. Medicines for depression or anxiety may be helpful. Talking to a mental health professional and your friends and family about the event and your feelings can also help. PTSD can cause depression and substance abuse. These problems should be treated before or during PTSD treatment.

How long does PTSD last?

PTSD can be treated successfully. However, without treatment, it can last several months to many years, depending on what happened to you and how you feel about it.

What can I do to help myself recover?

- Check your local phone directory for support groups in your area.

- Contact the Post Traumatic Stress Disorder Alliance.

- Learn more about PTSD, and work with your doctor or therapist to get better.

Suicide Prevention Lifeline

The National Suicide Prevention Lifeline has been enhanced with a new feature to provide a new service for veterans in crisis. Call 1-800-273-TALK (8255) and press 1 to be connected immediately to VA suicide prevention and mental health service professionals. Call for yourself, or someone you care about.

The National Suicide Prevention Lifeline
http:www.mentalhealth.va.gov

National Center for PTSD hotline
1-802-296-6300
http:www.ncptsd.va.gov/ncmain/index.jsp The NCPTSD website offers information about the symptoms, diagnosis and treatment of PTSD.

Department of Veterans Affairs   (VA)
1- 800 -827-1000
http://www.va.gov

Military One Source
1- 800- 342-9647
http:www.militaryonesource.com

BIBLE PROMISES FOR SOLDIERS

As you read these bible promises, meditate on them and memorize them. Confess these promises and make them your own. They will encourage and strengthen you. In the book of Daniel chapter 9 Daniel said, "I will pray to my God and make confessions. He will keep covenant, mercy and loving kindness with those who love him and keep his commandments." Daniel knew the value of confessing the word and he made it a part of his prayer time. I encourage you to do the same. Some of the verses of scripture are taken from the amplified version of the bible and personalized just for you. These promises will comfort you, uplift you, protect you and bring you peace during your time of war.

David's Song of Praise

2 Samuel Chapter 22

David sang to the LORD the words of this song when the LORD delivered him from the hand of all his enemies and from the hand of Saul.

He said: "The LORD is my rock, my fortress and my deliverer;

my God is my rock, in whom I take refuge, my shield and the horn of my salvation. He is my stronghold, my refuge and my savior from violent men you save me.

I call to the LORD, who is worthy of praise, and I am saved from my enemies.

"The waves of death swirled about me;

the torrents of destruction overwhelmed me.

The cords of the grave coiled around me; the snares of death confronted me.

In my distress I called to the LORD;

I called out to my God. From his temple he heard my voice; my cry came to his ears.

"The earth trembled and quaked,

the foundations of the heavens shook; they trembled because he was angry.

Smoke rose from his nostrils;

consuming fire came from his mouth,

burning coals blazed out of it.

He parted the heavens and came down;

dark clouds were under his feet.

He mounted the cherubim and flew;

he soared on the wings of the wind.

He made darkness his canopy around him the dark rain clouds of the sky.
Out of the brightness of his presence
bolts of lightning blazed forth.
The LORD thundered from heaven;
the voice of the Most High resounded.
He shot arrows and scattered the enemies, bolts of lightning and routed them.
The valleys of the sea were exposed
 and the foundations of the earth laid bare
 at the rebuke of the LORD, at the blast of breath from his nostrils.
"He reached down from on high and took hold of me; he drew me out of deep waters.
He rescued me from my powerful enemy, from my foes, who were too strong for me.
They confronted me in the day of my disaster, but the LORD was my support.
He brought me out into a spacious place; he rescued me because he delighted in me.
"The LORD has dealt with me
according to my righteousness;
according to the cleanness of my hands he has rewarded me.
For I have kept the ways of the LORD;
 I have not done evil by turning from my God.
All his laws are before me;
I have not turned away from his decrees.
I have been blameless before him
and have kept myself from sin.

The LORD has rewarded me according to my righteousness, according to my cleanness in his sight.
"To the faithful you show yourself faithful, to the blameless you show yourself blameless,
to the pure you show yourself pure,
but to the crooked you show yourself shrewd.
You save the humble,
but your eyes are on the haughty to bring them low.
You are my lamp, O LORD;
the LORD turns my darkness into light.
With your help I can advance against a troop; with my God I can scale a wall.
"As for God, his way is perfect;
the word of the LORD is flawless.
He is a shield for all who take refuge in him.
For who is God besides the LORD?
And who is the Rock except our God?
It is God who arms me with strength
and makes my way perfect.
He makes my feet like the feet of a deer; he enables me to stand on the heights.
He trains my hands for battle;
my arms can bend a bow of bronze.
You give me your shield of victory;
you stoop down to make me great.
You broaden the path beneath me,
so that my ankles do not turn.
"I pursued my enemies and crushed them; I did not turn back till they were destroyed.
I crushed them completely, and they could not rise; they fell beneath my feet.

You armed me with strength for battle;
you made my adversaries bow at my feet.
You made my enemies turn their backs in flight, and I
destroyed my foes.
They cried for help, but there was no one to save them to
the LORD, but he did not answer.
 I beat them as fine as the dust of the earth; I pounded
and trampled them like mud in the streets.
"You have delivered me from the attacks of my people;
you have preserved me as the head of nations. People I
did not know are subject to me,
and foreigners come cringing to me;
as soon as they hear me, they obey me.
They all lose heart; they come trembling from their
strongholds.
"The LORD lives! Praise be to my Rock! Exalted be God,
the Rock, my Savior!
He is the God who avenges me,
  who puts the nations under me,
who sets me free from my enemies.
You exalted me above my foes;
from violent men you rescued me.
Therefore I will praise you, O LORD, among the nations;
I will sing praises to your name.
He gives his king great victories;
he shows unfailing kindness to his anointed, to David
and his descendants forever."

PROTECTION

Psalm 3:3
But thou, O Lord, art a shield for me; my glory, and the lifter up of mine head.

Psalm 119: 116 *(Amplified bible)*
Uphold me according to your word, that I may live and do not let me be ashamed of my hope.

Psalm 119:77
Let your tender mercies come to me that I may live.

Psalm 119:146
Save me, and I will keep your testimonies.

Proverbs 18:10
The name of the Lord is a strong tower; the righteous run to it and are safe.

Exodus 23:20
Behold, I send an Angel before thee, to keep thee in the way, and to bring thee into the place, which I have prepared.

Exodus 23:22
As I obey your voice, and do all that you speak, be an enemy unto my enemies and an adversary unto my adversaries.

Psalm 59:1 *(Amplified bible)*
Deliver me from my enemies, O my God; Defend and protect me from those who rise up against me.

Psalm 91:1
He that dwelleth in the secret place of the Most High shall abide under the shadow of the Almighty.

Psalm 91:2
I will say of the Lord, he is my refuge and fortress, my God in him will I trust.

1Chronicles 4:10
Oh, that you would bless me and enlarge my border, and that your hand might be with me, and you would keep me from evil so it might not hurt me.

Psalm 61:3
For thou has been a shelter for me, a strong tower from the enemy.

Psalm 121:7
The Lord shall preserve me from all evil: He shall preserve my soul. The Lord shall preserve thy going out and thy coming in from this time forth, and even for evermore.

Psalm 119:114
Thou art my hiding place and my shield: I hope in thy word.

Isaiah 54:17
No weapon that is formed against me will prosper.

Isaiah 52:12
For you shall not go out with haste, nor go by flight: for the Lord will go before you; and the God of Israel will be your rearguard.

Psalm 91:7
A thousand may fall at thou side and ten thousand at thou right hand; but it shall not come nigh thee.

Psalm 27:35
Though an host should encamp against me, my heart shall not fear; though war should rise against me, in this I will be confident. For in the time of trouble he shall hide me in his pavilion; in the secret place of his tabernacle, he shall hide me; he shall set me upon a rock.

Psalm 34:7
The angel of the lord encamps round about them that fear him, and delivers them.

2 Chronicles 20:27
Lord made me to rejoice over my enemies

Jeremiah 39:18
I will save you; you will not fall by the sword but will escape with your life, because you trust in me, declares the Lord.

Psalm 91:10
There shall no evil will befall me, neither shall any plague come near my dwelling.

Psalm 143:9
Deliver me, O Lord, from my enemies.   In you I take shelter.

Psalm 103:1, 4
Bless the Lord, O my soul: and all that is within me, bless his holy name. Who redeems my life from destruction; who crown me with loving kindness and tender mercies.

Psalm 138:7
Though I walk in the midst of trouble, you will revive me; you will stretch forth your hand against the wrath of my enemies, and your right hand shall save me.

Job 5:20
In famine, he will redeem me from death, and in war from the power of the sword.

Psalm 140:7
O God, the strength of my salvation, you have covered my head in the day of battle.

2Kings 19:19
Now, O Lord my God, I pray, deliver us from his hand that all the Kingdoms of the earth may know that you alone, O Lord, are God.

Deuteronomy 3:24
O Lord God, you have begun to show your servant your greatness and your strong hand. For what god is there in heaven or on earth who can do such works and mighty acts as yours?

Psalm 68:18
Draw near to my soul, and redeem it; Deliver me because of my enemies.

Psalm 3: 7
Arise, O Lord; save me, O my God! For you have struck all my enemies on the cheek; You have broken the teeth of the ungodly.

Psalm 3:8
Salvation belongs to the Lord; May your blessing be upon your people.

Psalm 5: 8
Lead me, O Lord, in your righteousness because of my enemies; make your way straight before me.

Psalm 5:11
Let all who take refuge in you be glad, Let them ever sing for joy; and may you shelter them, that those who love your name may be joyful in you.

Psalm 5: 12
For it is you who blesses the righteous man, O Lord, you surround him with favor as with a shield.

Psalm 4:8
In will both lay down in peace, and sleep; for thou, Lord, only makes me dwell in safety.

Psalm 68:19-21
Blessed be the Lord, who daily bear our burden, The God who is our salvation. God is to us a God of deliverance; and to God the Lord belong escapes from death. Surely, God will shatter the head of his enemies, the hairy crown of him who goes on in his guilty deeds.

Psalm 71: 3
Be to me a rock of refuge in which to dwell, and a
sheltering stronghold to which I may continually resort,
which you have appointed to save me, for you are my
Rock and my Fortress.

Psalm 31: 15
My times are in your hands, deliver me from the hands
of my enemies and from those who persecute me.

COURAGE

Deuteronomy 33:27
The eternal God is your refuge, and underneath are the everlasting arms; He will thrust out the enemy from before you, and will say Destroy!

Psalm 27:14
I will wait on the Lord, and I will be of good courage and he shall strengthen my heart.

Deuteronomy 1: 29-30
Dread not, neither be afraid of them. The Lord your God which goes before you, he shall fight for you.

Joshua 1:9
Be strong and of good courage; do not be afraid, neither be thou dismayed, for the Lord your God is with you wherever thou go.

Psalm 3:6
I will not be afraid of ten thousands of people that have set themselves against me round about.

Psalm 56:11
In God have I put my trust: I will not be afraid what can man do unto me.

Romans 8:37
In all things, we are more than conquerors through him that loved us.

Psalm 60:12
Through God I will do valiantly, for He it is that shall tread down my enemies.

Judges 6:12
The Lord is with thee thou mighty man/woman of valor.

Psalm 18: 40
Thou have also given me the necks of my enemies, So that I destroyed those who hated me.

2 Timothy 1:7
For God has not given me a spirit of timidity (of cowardice, of craven and cringing and fawning fear), but he has given me a spirit of power and of love and of calm and well balanced mine and discipline and self-control.

Proverbs 21:31
The horse is prepared for the day of battle, but victory belongs to the Lord.

Psalm 24:8
Who is the King of Glory? The Lord strong and mighty, the Lord mighty in battle.

2 Chronicles 20:6
O Lord, the God of our fathers, are you not God in the heavens?   are you not ruler over all the kingdoms of the nations? Power and might are in your hand so that no one can stand against you.

Proverbs 28:1
The wicked flee when no one is pursuing, but the righteous are bold as a lion.

Isaiah 26:3
You will guard him and keep him in perfect and constant peace whose mind
(both its inclination and its character) is stayed on you, because he commits himself to you, lean on you, and hopes confidently in you.

COMFORT

Deuteronomy 20:4
For the Lord my God is he that goes with me, to fight for me against my enemies, to save me.

Psalm 121:1-2
I will lift mine eyes unto the hills, from whence cometh my help. My help comes from the Lord, which made heaven and earth.

Matthew 5: 9
I am blessed, because I am a peacemakers and I am called a child of God.

Isaiah 12:2
Behold, God is my salvation; I will trust, and not be afraid: for the Lord Jehovah is my strength and my song: he also has become my salvation.

Proverbs 3: 24
I will lie down, I will not be afraid, I shall lie down and my sleep will be sweet.

Proverbs 3: 25-26
I will be not afraid of sudden fear and panic, nor of the stormy blast and ruin of the wicked when it comes. For the Lord shall by my confidence, and shall keep my foot from being taken.

Psalm 60: 4
Thou hast given a banner to them that fear thee, that it may be displayed because of the truth.

Psalm 118:17
I shall not die, but live, and declare the works of the Lord.

2 Corinthian 2:14
Now thanks be unto God, which always causes us to triumph in Christ, and maketh manifest the savour of his knowledge by us in every place.

Isaiah 41:10
Fear not, for I am with you, be not dismayed, for I am your God, I will strength thee, yea, I will help thee; yea, I will uphold thee with the right hand of my righteousness.

Joshua 1:5
There shall not any man be able to stand before thee all the days of thy life; as I was with Moses, so I will be with thee. I will not fail thee, nor forsake thee.

Genesis 28:15
Behold I am with thee, and will keep thee in all places whither thou goest, and will bring thee again into this land; for I will not leave you until I have done what I have spoken to you.

Psalm 23:4
Yea thou I walk through the valley of the shadow of death, I will fear no evil for you are with me.

Deuteronomy 7: 21
I shall not dread them, for the Lord my God is in my midst, a great and awesome God.

Deuteronomy 7: 23
The Lord will deliver them before you, and will throw them into great confusion until they are destroyed.

Numbers 10:9
When you go to war in your land against the adversary who attacks you, then you shall sound an alarm with the trumpets, that you may be remembered before the Lord your God, and be saved from your enemies.

John 14:27
Peace, I leave with you; my peace I give to you; not as the world gives do it give to you. Do not let your heart be troubled, nor let it be fearful.

STRENGTH

Psalm 28:7
The Lord is my Strength and my shield; my heart trusted in him and I am helped. Therefore my heart greatly rejoice: and with my song will I praise him.

Psalm 144:1
Blessed be the Lord my strength, which teaches my hands to war, and my fingers to fight.

Psalm 59:17
Unto thee, O my strength, I will sing; for God is my defense, and the God of my mercy.

Psalm 62:7
In God is my salvation and my glory: the rock of my strength and my refuge, is in God.

Psalm 18:39
For you have girded me with strength for the battle you have subdued under me those that rose up against me.

Psalm 18:37
I have pursued mine enemies, and overtaken them: neither did I turn again until they were consumed.

Ephesians 6:10
Finally, my brethren be strong in the lord and in the power of his might. Put on the whole armor of God.

Psalm 140:7
O God the Lord, the strength of my salvation, you have covered my head in the day of battle.

Psalm 46:1
God is our refuge and strength, a very present help in trouble.

Joshua 14:11
As my strength was then even so is my strength now, for war, both to go out and to come in.

Psalm 18: 34
The Lord teaches my hands to make war, so that my arms can bend a bow of bronze.

Psalm 18:29
For by thee I have run through a troop; and by my God I can leaped over a wall.

Deuteronomy 33: 29
The Lord is the shield of your help, and the sword of your majesty! Your enemies shall submit to you, and you shall tread down their high places.

Judges 5: 31
So may all your enemies parish, O Lord! But may they who love you be like the sun when it rises in it's strength.

Psalm 17:7
Wondrously show your lovingkindness, O Savior of those who take refuge at your right hand from those who rise up against them.

Psalm 17:8

Keep me as the apple of your eye; Hide me in the shadow of your wings from the wicked who despoil me, my deadly enemies who surround me. They have closed their unfeeling heart, with their mouth they speak proudly.

Psalm 17

11 They have surrounded us in our steps; They set their eyes to cast us down to the ground.

12 He is like a lion that is eager to tear, and as a young lion lurking in hiding places.

13 Arise, O Lord, confront him, bring him low; Deliver my life from the wicked with your sword.

Zechariah 10: 5

We will be as mighty men, treading down the enemy in the mire of the streets of battle.

Psalm 89: 22-23

The enemy shall not outwit me, Nor the son of wickedness afflict me, I will beat down my foe before his face and plague those who hate me.

Galatians 6:9

I will not lose heart and grow weary and faint in acting nobly and doing right, for in due time and at the appointed season I shall reap, if I do not loosen and relax my courage and faint.

THE AUTHOR

J.M. Barnes is a native of Tampa, Florida. She was a military spouse for over 20 years. She is an educator, an author and mother of 3 children. She is a graduate of Saint Leo University. She has two degrees and is currently attending the University of West Florida pursuing her Master's degree.

To contact the author, write:

J.M. Barnes

P.O. Box 364

Christmas, FL. 32709

www. biblepromisesforsoldiers.blogspot.com

LaVergne, TN USA
05 August 2010
192201LV00001B/1/P